GW01605962

Bentzi

and the Abandoned House

Printed in E.Israel

Layout: Goldblatt 972-5000845

Bentzi and the Abandoned House

1. Summer Adventure 1
2. Nadav and Chemda 8
3. A Spy 16
4. Hidden Treasure 23
5. Treasure Hunt 30
6. Stepping Stones 37
7. Rescue 44
8. Bedridden 51
9. Once upon a Time 58
10. What Nadav Found 65
11. A Riddle 73
12. Fishing 80
13. The Spreader of Light 87
14. A Strange Idea 94
15. To the Abandoned House 101
16. The Treasure 108
17. The Mystery Solved 115
18. The Real Alexander Stone 122

1. Summer Adventure

There's something mysterious and thrilling about an abandoned house, don't you think? And if you add a treasure hunt as well — untold riches hidden away, nobody knows where — you end up with a really exciting adventure.

Bentzi's secret club would have had great fun, no doubt, but his club wasn't in Silver Brook Village during those happy summer days. Just Bentzi and Tova and I. Imagine!

And it all started just when summer vacation, which had been so exciting when it was new and full of promise, began to feel dreary and boring and stretched out. Day camp was over, and there was nothing to fill the long days that seemed never to end. At least we could borrow books from the library! If you've read *Bentzi to the Rescue*, you know not to take that for granted.

But there weren't enough new books in the library, and even after Tova and I helped Mommy with the housework, and had some baking and cooking sessions with her, and took Moishy and Shmuel to the playground — we still had lots of empty, boring time on our hands. We almost envied Bentzi, who still went to school each morning. Of course, he himself could hardly wait for his own summer vacation to start.

"Vacation is boring," Tova warned him, but Bentzi just said, "Well, maybe mine will be interesting."

And at that moment Mommy came into the room, all smiles. "Surprise!" she announced. "Bubby and Zaidy are going to the country for a week, to a place called Silver Brook Village, and they want you to come along!"

"Really?" "Wow!" "When do we start?" "Where is Silver Brook?" "I can't believe it!" "Are all of us going?"

Of all the exclamations and questions, Mommy chose to reply to the last one. "Not all of you. Only the older kids."

Only the older ones! Bentzi and I exchanged excited glances. But I am kindhearted and unselfish. I didn't think only of my own pleasure; there was room in my heart for my disappointed little sister as well. Poor Tova! I turned to her and said softly: "Never mind, Tova. Maybe you'll get a chance like this some other time."

"What?" Tova stared at me as if I were speaking

Chinese. "Never mind what? What other time? I'm coming along this time!"

"But only the older kids are going, didn't you hear?" I explained patiently. "Bentzi and I are the older kids, and you — that is, Moishy, Shmuel and you — are the little ones."

"No! Moishy and Shmuel are the little ones. I'm one of the big ones!"

"She's the middle child," said Bentzi, "Sometimes she's one of the big ones, and sometimes one of the little ones. Right, Mommy?"

"Right," Mommy agreed, patting Tova's shoulder. "And this time you're one of the big ones, Tova dear. Bubby invited you too."

Tova beamed. Mommy tried to calm the wailing Moishy and Shmuel, and Bentzi got out a map and tried to locate Silver Brook Village.

As for me, I hurried to the phone to call Esti. "You'll never guess what happened!"

"Then tell me," she requested reasonably.

"Are you listening?"

"Yes."

"So, listen to this—"

"I already told you I'm listening!" Esti interrupted.

"Okay, okay, just let me tell you. Bentzi and Tova and I are going to the country for a week!"

"Really? Lucky you. Who will you be staying with?"

"My grandparents."

"You never told me your grandparents lived in the country!"

"They don't. They live here in town, but they're going to the country for a week, to stay in Silver Brook Village, and they're taking us along."

Ahhh... Silver Brook... What a lovely name! It makes me think of swimming in cool blue water, or swinging in a hammock in the shade of a tree, to

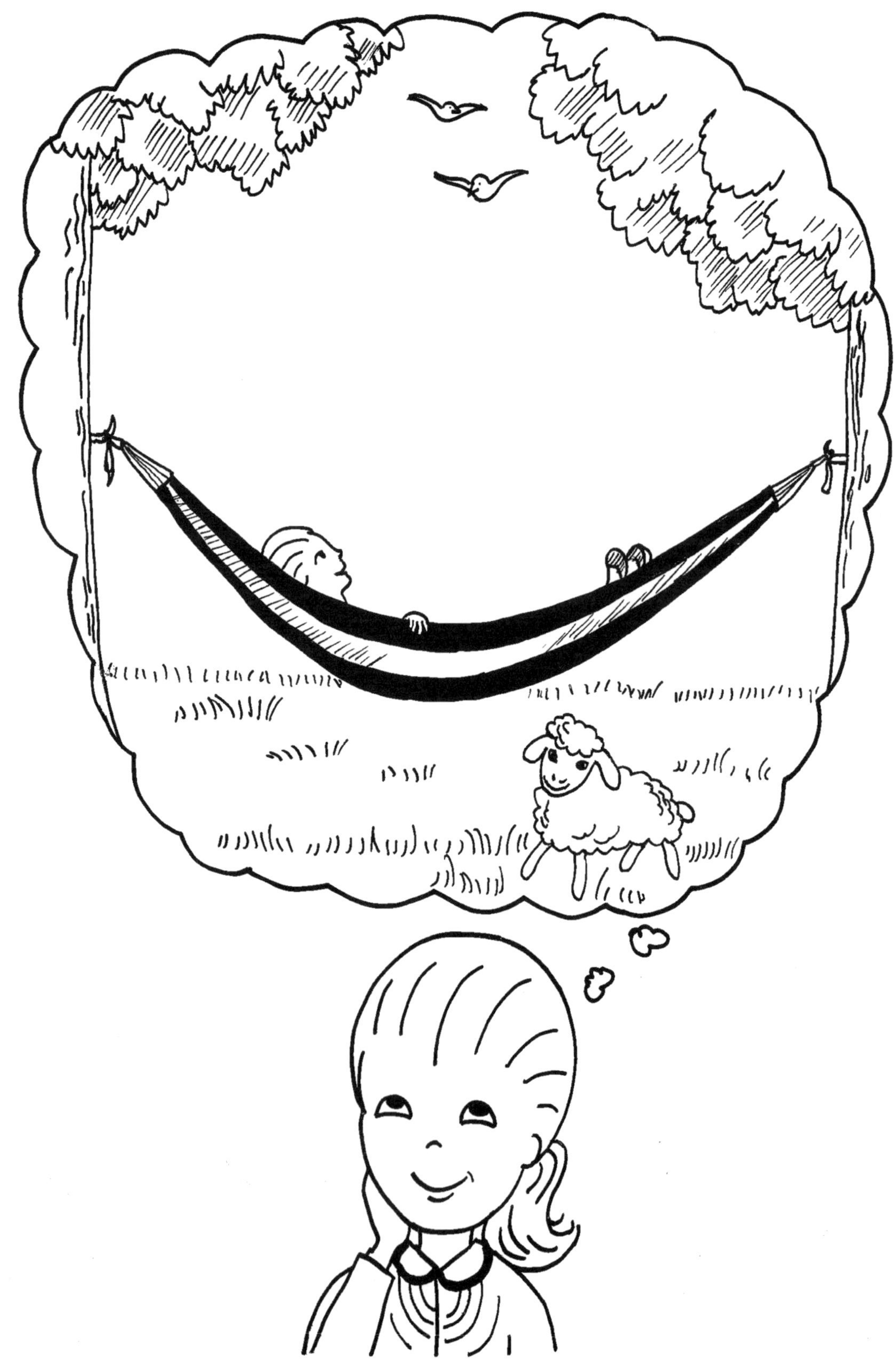

the musical cooing of doves and the soft bleating of lambs.

"It will all be so quiet and peaceful," I said dreamily.

"I just hope it won't be **too** quiet and peaceful," said Bentzi, suddenly alarmed.

He needn't have worried.

2. Nadav and Chemda

Did you ever notice how slowly time crawls along when you're waiting for something? It's maddening! But even slow crawling gets you there eventually, and we finally found ourselves sitting in a van with Bubby and Zaidy and piles of luggage, on our way to the country.

"At last! I can hardly believe it!" said Bentzi, jumping up and down on the seat beside me.

Zaidy grinned at us. "You'll have a good time

out there."

"Yes," said Bubby. "It's the loveliest place in the world, at least according to Amalya."

"Who's Amalya?" I asked.

"A friend of mine from work," Bubby explained.

My grandmother works in a big office, something to do with taxes. I don't understand exactly what she does, but she works hard all year round, and really needs a vacation. Sometimes I wish she was more like grandmothers in stories, who knit sweaters and bake cookies, and are always home and have time to listen to their grandchildren's stories about school and friends and whatever.

But why am I complaining? Bubby's on vacation now, and she'll be with us all day long!

"How does Amalya know it's the loveliest place in the world?" asked Tova. "Did she ever go there on vacation?"

"No, never," Zaidy answered, hiding a smile under his moustache.

"Then how does she know, if she was never there?"

Zaidy's smile widened. "I didn't say she was never there. I said she never went there on vacation. Know why? Because she lives there."

"Really?All year round? Lucky her!"

"Well, it's not so easy," said Bubby. "It's a long way to the office and back every day. But Amalya and her husband and the twins love Silver Brook. They won't hear of moving. They have a big house with a garden, and at the bottom of the garden there's a little house that they rent to people who come on vacation. That means us!"

"Twins? Boys or girls?" I asked. "And how old?"

"A boy and a girl, about your age," Bubby said. "A little younger than you, a little older than Bentzi.

You can make friends with them."

"What about me?" asked Tova. "Don't they have a girl my age too? Just big kids?"

"When you wanted to come along on this vacation, you said you're one of the big kids," I reminded her.

"That's not the same— —," she began, but Bentzi cut her off with a shout: "Here it is! Look, this sign says Silver Brook Village!"

Everything was just as I had pictured it. Wide stretches of green grass, a candy-striped hammock in the shade of a spreading tree, and the dearest little house with a red roof. Inside was a bedroom for Bubby and Zaidy, another bedroom with a bunk bed for Tova and me, and a larger room that was kitchen and living room in one, with a couch in the corner for Bentzi to sleep on.

We all helped Bubby unpack, and then she

began preparing dinner. Zaidy went to look for the nearest shul, and we went out into the garden. Bentzi found a good tree for climbing, and Tova and I took turns swinging in the hammock, counting to a hundred each time.

I was chanting "Sixty-one, sixty-two" and swinging Tova back and forth, when I heard a voice behind me: "Hi! Are you my mother's friend's grandchildren?"

It was a girl of about my age, with two bright red braids and a freckle-sprinkled face.

"Yes," I answered. "And you must be my grandmother's friend's daughter."

She nodded. "My name is Chemda, and this is Nadav, my twin." She pointed at Bentzi's tree. Among the branches, beside Bentzi's dark-haired head, a bright red one glowed.

"Come on, Nadav's taking us on a tour of the village!" Bentzi called out, sliding down the trunk and landing at our feet. "He'll show us the sheep and cows and all."

The village was gorgeous! Each house was built in a different style, with various parts painted in different colors. A pink fence here, a green door or purple shutters there. Not at all like the apartment buildings of Springhill, which all look exactly the same.

And there was something to see in every front yard. A lawn mower, a playpen fitted with a handle and large wheels for riding through the village, even a little goldfish pond.

"See the cactuses?" said Nadav, pointing at a yard filled with cactuses in all sizes and shapes.

"And those adorable dolls with the funny hats!" exclaimed Tova, stopping in front of another yard.

"They're garden gnomes," Chemda told her. One gnome had a miniature rake in its hand,

another had a small watering can, and a third held the handles of a doll-sized wheelbarrow.

And then we passed a house with nothing but overgrown brambles in its front yard. Empty windows stared out at us like blank, unseeing eyes.

"What's this house? Why is it like this?" asked Bentzi.

"Oh, that," said Nadav. "That's the abandoned house."

3. A Spy

"The abandoned house?" asked Bentzi. "What do you mean? Why is it abandoned? Who abandoned it? Why?"

"Ah!" said Nadav, smiling mysteriously. "That's a long story. Long and thrilling. Want to hear it now?"

"Yes!" said Bentzi, still looking at the empty windows, the paint flaking off the door, the bramble-choked yard. I could almost hear the wheels whirring in his mind: Was this house a headquarters for missionaries, or perhaps for smugglers? Was it used for hiding stolen goods? Bentzi knows a lot about hiding stolen goods, as you may remember from *Bentzi's Secret Club*.

"But I want to go see the cows now!" Tova protested.

Chemda took her hand and skipped ahead, her carroty braids swinging briskly behind her. "Come, Tova. To the barn! There'll be plenty of time later for Nadav's stories."

A moment later we were at the barn. Somehow the cows seemed bigger than I had expected, and when one of them turned her enormous eyes on me and let out a sudden loud "Moooo," I stepped backward in alarm.

"Want to see the calves, Tova?" I quickly suggested. While Chemda fed stalks of grass to a huge cow, we slipped away to a small fenced-

in corner of the barn and admired the cute little calves.

Bentzi soon joined us, but the calves didn't interest him much. "Batya, what do you think the story of the abandoned house could be?" he asked.

"Oh, Nadav was just fooling," I said. "Don't get your hopes up. Probably the owner just doesn't feel like living out here. It's a great place, and you can see why Amalya loves it so much, but, after all, most people prefer living in town."

"What's that got to do with anything?" said Bentzi. "He doesn't have to live here. He can sell the house, or rent it to someone, and get lots of money. Why let it stand empty and useless?"

That made sense, I had to admit. Really, why not sell or rent the house? Maybe there was some mysterious reason after all.

Tova wanted to go see the sheep too, but it

was getting late. "Bubby made lunch and she's expecting us back," I said.

"We can go see the sheep in the afternoon," said Chemda. "I'm so glad you're here! I was starting to feel bored with this long vacation."

"Me too," I told her. "But I'm sure we won't be bored here." And I wasn't thinking just of the village and all the interesting things to see. I was thinking of Chemda herself as well. Surely we'd have lots of fun with such a friend right next door.

"Tell us the story now, Nadav," said Bentzi.

So while we walked home through paths that wound lazily past trees and bushes and colorful fences, Nadav told us the story of the abandoned house.

"I don't know if it's true," he said, "but this is what the village kids say. A man called Alexander Stone used to live in that house, and he was—" Nadav paused for dramatic effect before finishing solemnly, "—a spy."

"A spy?" Bentzi's eyes shone. "A real spy right here in Silver Brook Village? Did you know him?"

"Oh, no, that was before I was born. Alexander used to go on secret, dangerous missions to hostile countries, and in between he would come and rest at home in this quiet village."

"Did his family live here?" asked Bentzi.

"He didn't have a family. He didn't want to get married and have children, because of his dangerous job. He never knew if he would get home safely from a mission."

"Now tell them about the treasure," urged Chemda.

"Treasure? What treasure?" Bentzi, Tova and I all asked together.

"Don't rush me. I was just getting to that," said Nadav.

But here we were at our gate already, and

a delicious smell wafted towards us from the window of the little red-roofed house. "Bubby's special meatballs!" cried Tova.

"With yellow rice and tomato sauce!" I guessed, sniffing the air. Suddenly I felt terribly hungry.

Chemda flashed us an understanding smile. "City kids always get appetites in Silver Brook. My mother says it's the fresh air. Well, the treasure's been waiting around for years; I guess it'll keep till after lunch."

4. Hidden Treasure

After a fabulous lunch we helped Bubby clear up and wash the dishes, and then we went out in the garden. The twins were already waiting for us on the garden swing next to the big house. Bubby sat down in a wicker chair with a book, and we hurried over to hear the rest of the story of Alexander Stone, Silver Brook's very own spy.

To the smell of freshly cut grass and the caress of a light breeze, Nadav told us that Alexander had been very rich. The CIA paid him well for his high-risk work, and he hardly spent any money, living quietly by himself in a small village. He had a lot of money saved up, and his problem was deciding where to keep it.

At this point you must be wondering: What's the problem? Money goes in the bank!

The thing is, Alexander Stone was a suspicious type. He didn't trust banks, or anyone else for that matter. As a spy he was used to deceiving people, pretending he was just a clerk or a tourist, while in fact he was trying to discover important state secrets. And so he always suspected others of trying to deceive him. This often happens — when people act a certain way, they suspect others of doing the same.

Alexander decided to hide his property in a special hiding place, where nobody would think of looking. Because he spent so much time abroad, thieves could take advantage of the times when the house was empty. So he had to find a place where they wouldn't think to look.

He used all his money to buy diamonds ("Just like the mean neighbor in *Yosef Mokir Shabbos,"* Tova whispered to me) and hid them in a secret place he told no one about.

And then it happened: Alexander Stone was killed while on a dangerous mission. The treasure stayed hidden away in its secret place till this very day, and the house remained empty and abandoned. Nobody wanted to come live in a house whose owner had met with such a tragic death.

As soon as Nadav finished his story, Bentzi let fly with his questions: "How was he killed? Did they discover he was a spy and execute him? And where did he hide the treasure? Inside the abandoned house? And why won't anyone live there? What has that got to do with his being killed? I mean, he wasn't killed because of the house, was he?"

Nadav shrugged. "I guess that's how people feel, even if it doesn't make sense. And I don't know exactly how he was killed. As for the treasure — some say it's hidden in the house, others say it's somewhere else in the village. I don't know who's right. Maybe nobody's right. I don't even know if this whole story is true at all, but that's the story they tell about the abandoned house."

The purple door of the big house opened suddenly, and Amalya appeared in the doorway. "Nadav! Chemda! You ran away right after lunch, without clearing the table and washing the dishes!"

The twins got up reluctantly and went inside, leaving us to bask in the sweet satisfaction of having helped in the house before going out to have fun.

"If I found a treasure of diamonds and precious stones," said Bentzi dreamily, "like in books, where kids always find treasure chests on desert islands — first of all I'd set up a charity, and save people from dire poverty. And then… Then I'd buy a new bike."

"I'd buy a camera," I said. "I've wanted a camera of my own for ages."

"I want the swimming lessons that Daddy said were too expensive," said Tova, "and lots and lots of candy!"

"And what'll we get for Mommy?" I asked. "How about a dishwasher?"

Bentzi laughed. "That's really for you, so you won't have to take your turn washing dishes… Better get her some jewelry or something. For Moishy and Shmuel we can get a big toy garage with lots of cars."

"Yes, and a rocking horse!" cried Tova. "Like I saw at my friend Ilana's house, all soft and velvety, just like a real horse!"

We spent several more pleasant minutes planning gifts for Daddy, our friends, and of course Bubby and Zaidy, who had brought us to this village of hidden treasure.

"But of course we'll never find it," I finally reminded Bentzi and Tova, shattering all our delightful fantasies. "This whole story about the spy might not even be true, and even if it is — how would we know where to search for the treasure, after years and years of nobody finding it?"

5. Treasure Hunt

In the afternoon, we set out to seek the treasure.

"You're right, we probably won't find anything," Bentzi told me, "but what can we lose by trying? Back home there aren't any abandoned houses, or treasures hidden away by brave spies. Let's make the most of it while we're here."

Nadav and Chemda had no such consideration, of course, but they were glad to join us. "To the abandoned house!" cried Chemda merrily, skipping along, her braids swinging behind her.

Tova slipped her hand into mine. "Are you scared, Batya?"

"Of course not!" I laughed, but clasped her hand tightly. An abandoned house, empty and mysterious, perhaps concealing an old treasure. A spy sent on a dangerous mission, never to return. There was nothing to be afraid of, but still…

"Here we are!" Nadav announced. The abandoned house stood before us, much less scary in reality than it had been in my imagination. The yard was neglected and the door needed painting, but it was really just an empty house and nothing more.

The gate was open, but the front door was locked. "It's not a good idea to go inside an empty house anyway," said Nadav, "but we can search out here. What do you think, Bentzi? Could the treasure be hidden in the yard?"

"You can never tell," said Bentzi importantly. He rummaged among some old boxes that were piled in the corner, then peered between the bushes. "In books you always dig to find treasures," he added a little less confidently. He found a sharp-pointed branch and tried to dig, but managed to do little more than scratch the hard ground.

"I could go get a shovel," said Nadav, "but what for? This won't work. In books you don't dig just anywhere. You always have a map or clues or something showing where the treasure is buried."

"So let's leave this abandoned house and go see the sheep," suggested Tova.

Bentzi decided he'd rather go for a bike ride around the village with Nadav.

"Let's go home and get my bike," said Nadav, "and I'll borrow one from the neighbors for you."

Chemda, Tova and I spent a pleasant hour with the soft, woolly sheep. When we tired of that, Chemda asked, "Want to go to the brook?"

"Is there a brook around here?"

"Of course! That's why it's called Silver Brook Village. Come on, it'll be fun there."

It was fun on the way too. Tova kept darting off in all directions, picking flowers and chasing butterflies, while Chemda and I walked and talked together. Chemda told me about the little village school. Just imagine — there are only five girls in her class! Once all the other four didn't come, and Chemda had two private lessons before the teacher finally let her go home!

I told her about our big school with all the parallel classes. "It's a pity we're only here for a few days," I said. "We could have been friends."

"So let's write to each other!" said Chemda eagerly. "I always wanted a pen pal."

"Me too! I even tried it with Esti, my friend who lives nearby, but we didn't keep it up. It feels silly writing to someone you see every day. But you and I can be pen pals, that's a great idea!"

As we talked, we passed the last house at the edge of the village. Tova ran towards us, waving a bunch of wild flowers and crying excitedly: "I can hear the brook!"

I stopped to listen. Yes! I could hear the gurgling sound of water in the distance. Chemda led us to the serenely flowing brook. What a refreshing sight! Suddenly I realized how hot I was after our long walk. We dipped our hands in the cool water and washed our faces, then sat down to rest beside the brook.

"Look at those pretty blue flowers," said Tova, pointing at the far side of the brook. "I'm making a bouquet for Bubby, and I don't have any blues yet. Just yellows and whites."

"So come on, let's pick some blue ones," said Chemda, jumping up.

"What?" We both stared at her in surprise. "But how can we get to the other side?"

6. Stepping Stones

"Easy," said Chemda, pointing to several large stones that rose above the surface of the water. "See? These are stepping stones. You go from one to the other, and you reach the other side in a flash!" She skipped with surprising ease from stepping stone to stepping stone, and waved at us cheerfully from the opposite bank. "Come on!"

We didn't budge. "It looks dangerous," I said.

"Nonsense," Chemda called out. "It's easy as

can be, there's nothing to be scared of. And there are so many gorgeous blue flowers here!"

Tova approached the brook gingerly, hesitated, then strode bravely from stone to stone, finally stepping onto the opposite bank. "Now you, Batya," she called out. "Come on, it really is easy. It only looks scary before you try."

I looked at the flowing water, rushing by so quickly. Why had I ever thought it was serene? How did Tova do it? The stones seemed so far away from each other, and such irregular shapes, and one of them was so small! I could easily slip and fall into the water. I was afraid, and besides, I didn't want Chemda and Tova to see me falling. I didn't want them to see I couldn't cross the brook easily, just like them.

"I'll wait for you here," I said.

"Okay," said Tova, turning to pick blue flowers. But Chemda refused to give up. "Come on, Batya.

It's nothing, really! What are you scared of? Do it once and you'll see it's nothing."

"Yes, but I… I'm not good at this kind of thing. My mark in gym class always spoils my report card," I explained, shuddering as I thought of my failed attempts to climb the ropes dangling from the gym ceiling, or to jump over the horse.

"But this isn't a gym exercise, it's just plain stepping from one stone to another. Just do it already, Batya," Chemda urged. "It's fun!"

I looked at her face smiling at me encouragingly from between her bright braids, and I knew I had no choice. I couldn't disappoint Chemda. If I kept on sitting there like a baby, she wouldn't want to be my friend anymore. She wouldn't want to keep in touch with me and be my pen pal like we had planned.

Okay. This was it. I took a deep breath and extended a cautious foot toward the first stone.

Now the other foot — Oh, no! I had left the safe bank behind, and was standing alone on a small, slippery stone in the middle of a rushing brook!

"Go on!" Chemda called. "Don't stop. It's easier to cross quickly than slowly."

What? Oh. Cross quickly! All at once I unfroze and ran onwards, to the next stepping stone. My foot hit it, twisted, and — oops! — stumbled and slipped off it.

This would be a good place to end the chapter and leave you in suspense till the next chapter. But if I do that, this chapter will be too short... So I'll go on.

I found myself standing in cold water up to my knees, and with a sharp pain in my foot. "Ow!" I shrieked in alarm. I waded toward the other side, accompanied by Chemda's and Tova's anxious cries. With each step the pain grew worse.

Tova and Chemda stretched out their hands to

help me climb out. I clung to Tova's hands and climbed out, hurt and ashamed, ignoring Chemda and her outstretched hands. That Chemda… Why did she do this to me? I told her I wasn't good at this sort of thing. Why didn't she listen? Why did she pester me so? It's her fault I fell, her fault I made a fool of myself, her fault I'm soaking wet and my foot hurts so badly.

"Oh, Batya, I'm so sorry. I never thought you'd fall in," said Chemda, her freckles standing out on her suddenly white face. "Besides, the water isn't at all deep. If it was, I wouldn't have told you to try. I'm so very sorry!"

Her apologies only made me madder. So what if the water wasn't deep? It was dangerous anyway! Maybe I had even broken a bone, and all because of her!

"Something happened to my foot," I told Tova, trying not to cry in front of Chemda. "I don't know how I'll get home.”

"I'll run and get help,” Chemda volunteered immediately. "I'll knock at the nearest house and ask to call home. My mother will know what to do. Bye, I'll be right back!"

She crossed the brook at a run, skimming once more with amazing ease over those terrible stepping stones, and soon disappeared from our sight.

7. Rescue

We sat down to wait for Chemda. "Lucky it's so hot," said Tova, trying to cheer me up. "If it were cold, you'd feel awful in these wet clothes."

"I feel awful in them anyhow!" I whined. "They cling and itch, and my foot..."

"Does it hurt real bad?" Tova asked anxiously.

Instead of answering, I asked, "When will Chemda come back?" as though Tova could know the answer. "I want Mommy," I added, and wiped my eyes on my wet sleeve, which didn't do much good.

Tova looked at me helplessly. I knew I sounded like a baby, but I didn't care. I wished I were at home with Mommy. She would know what to do.

A small, logical voice in my mind said: "If you were home now — you wouldn't have fallen into the brook, and Mommy wouldn't have to know what to do." I ignored the voice and went right on pitying myself. Chemda had said her mother would know what to do, but I didn't want Chemda's mother. I wanted **my** mother.

Tova shaded her eyes with her hand and looked out over the brook. "I don't see Chemda yet," she said, "but I bet she'll be here in a minute."

I never knew that a foot could hurt so badly, or that a minute could be so long! Maybe Chemda had forgotten we were waiting there with a broken ankle or something of the sort, and she was swinging away happily in the hammock or garden swing with a glass of icy lemonade, and we would wait out there all night, and… "Here she is!" cried Tova. Chemda's small figure was approaching on the far side of the brook, calling to us from afar, "My father's coming in the car to get you!"

She skipped from stepping stone to stepping stone until she stood beside us, trying to catch her breath. "You'll have to walk only till the road, Batya. Can you do it? Want to lean on my arm?"

"No, thanks. I'll manage," I answered in a voice as chilly as the water I had fallen into. I got up and tried to walk a few steps, but the pain grew suddenly sharper, and I had to lean on Tova and hop on one foot till we got to the road.

An old white car was already waiting for us there, and I collapsed onto the back seat with relief. Mommy wasn't there, of course, but Bubby was. She hugged me just like Mommy and whispered reassuringly, "Batya dear, does your foot hurt very badly? Don't worry, soon the doctor will take care of it and it won't hurt anymore. Everything will be all right."

"I'm taking you straight to the clinic," said Chemda's father, and stepped on the gas.

Silver Brook's clinic was just like our clinic at home — white walls, abstract paintings, blue metal chairs. And the smell was the same too — clean and artificial, very different from the smell of hay and flowers and chickens outside. The receptionist lifted her glance from the keyboard when we came in and said, "What can I do for you?

"My granddaughter fell and hurt her foot," Bubby explained.

"The doctor will see her shortly," said the receptionist. "Wait here, please."

Oh, no! More waiting? But we hadn't been

sitting for long on the blue chairs when my name was called, and we went into the doctor's office. She examined my foot and sent me for an x-ray.

Did you ever have an x-ray taken? It's a little scary. The technician covered me with a heavy lead apron and aimed a machine at my foot. Then he left the room, and I was alone with the pain. But I didn't feel the actual x-ray at all, and soon I was back on a blue chair in the reception area, waiting apprehensively for the diagnosis. Was this how defendants in court feel while awaiting their sentence?

"It's not broken," the doctor announced at last, "only sprained. I'll bandage your foot, and then you must stay in bed and rest. Don't walk any more than absolutely necessary."

"Boruch Hashem, it's not broken!" Bubby sighed with relief. But I asked anxiously, "How long will it take?"

"Hard to tell. A few days."

"But we're only here on vacation for a few days!" I wailed. "It's not fair!"

We got into Chemda's father's car and drove home, and all the while the words were shouting over and over in my mind: Not fair! Not fair!

All those long days at the end of the school year I was perfectly healthy. Every morning, when I would have loved to stay in bed instead of hurrying off to school, nothing hurt. And now, on these special days of vacation in the country, days that were supposed to be full of walks and adventures and exciting treasure hunts — now I would have to stay in bed and miss all the fun.

Can you believe it?

8. Bedridden

"Tweet-tweet!" Huh? Why do I hear chirping so close by? Did a bird get into my room? I opened my eyes and saw a tree just outside my window. Several birds perched on its branches, merrily chirping away.

For a moment I was confused. What was a tree doing right outside my window? Then I remembered: I wasn't at home. I was on vacation in the country, and today would be a magical, fun-

filled day! And then I tried to jump out of bed, and a stabbing pain in my foot brought back all that had happened the day before: the brook, the fall, the clinic, the x-ray. And finally, the doctor's verdict: Stay in bed for a few days.

I flopped back onto the bed and hid my face in the pillow. Yes, I was on vacation in the country, but what good was that? No magical, fun-filled day lay before me. What awaited me was a long, boring day of lying in bed indoors. Bentzi and Tova would explore the village, climb trees, feed hens, ride donkeys or horses, maybe even find the treasure, while I was stuck here with my injured foot.

Those of you who have counted the days till your vacation in the country, and then fell into a brook and sprained your ankle on your very first day there, will know exactly how I felt.

I heard steps approaching my bed, and raised

my head from the pillow. Bentzi and Tova stood gravely in front of me. "Batya, we're staying home with you today!" Tova declared. Bentzi placed a hand over his heart. "We cannot go out seeking pleasure while you are confined to your bed," he said solemnly.

The truth is it felt good to hear that. I was glad to see that my brother and sister were willing to give up their fun so as not to leave me alone, bored and unhappy.

But I refused, of course. "Thanks, you're the greatest! But I don't want you to miss out because of me," I said. "Bad enough that I have to spend the day in bed. At least you can have a good time."

"Batya's right," Bubby called from the kitchen. "It's lovely that you're willing to stay with her all day, but it's not necessary. Batya will manage all right. I'll be with her, and maybe Chemda will drop in."

Chemda? Oh, no! Yesterday's hot resentment boiled up in me again. This was all because of Chemda! It was her fault that I was in bed with a hurt and bandaged foot, her fault that my vacation was coming to nothing. All her fault! Why did she have to urge me to cross the brook, till I felt ashamed to refuse? Why couldn't she have left me sitting in peace on the bank like I wanted, instead of trying to cross over on those slippery stones?

"I don't want Chemda to come," I said quickly.

"Why not?" Bubby asked in surprise. "She's so nice. You had a good time with her yesterday, didn't you?"

I had. At least at first. But now I didn't want to see her anymore. "I'm too tired for visitors," I said. "I just want to rest."

"Whatever you say," Bubby agreed calmly. But I could tell she was puzzled. Well, I guess it did sound weird. After all, I wasn't sick, and my foot only hurt if I tried to walk. I should have welcomed the idea of a friend coming to sit with me and help pass the time. But I wasn't going to talk to that Chemda!

The morning dragged slowly by. When Zaidy went to shul to learn, and Bentzi and Tova went out to see more of the village's wonders, only Bubby and I were left in the little house. I talked to Mommy and Daddy on the phone, telling them I was fine and not to worry. Then I called Esti and told her everything that had happened. But I didn't mention Chemda. I didn't want to think about her.

"Maybe if I help you, you can hop out to sit in the yard?" Bubby suggested. I wished I could, but what would I do if Chemda came out into the yard? With this foot I wouldn't be able to get away… I shook my head.

"So how about reading a book?" asked Bubby. "If

you didn't bring along any books, maybe Chemda could lend you one."

"No, I don't feel like reading now. Let's just talk. You're always so busy, Bubby, we never have time to just sit and talk."

Bubby laughed. She pulled a chair over and sat down by my bed. "You're right, Batya. It's a rare opportunity! So what do you want to talk about?"

9. Once upon a Time

It was a good question. What could we talk about? Usually I chatter along nonstop; just ask my teachers! But now I suddenly had nothing to say.

The thing is, Bubby and I don't really talk a lot usually. I already told you how busy she is. She's not like the grandmothers you read about in books, who always have time to fill jars with delicious homemade cookies and sit down for heart-to-heart talks with the grandkids. Maybe that's why I suddenly felt shy now.

"Tell me stories from when you were my age," I said at last, "what life was like back then."

Bubby laughed. "What can I tell you? I didn't draw water from the well or wash clothes in a tub... We had a refrigerator and washing machine and even a telephone. Not a cellphone, of course, not even a cordless phone. We had a phone with a round dial that was plugged into the wall."

"So what did you do if you were out and needed to call someone?"

"Oh, we survived somehow, even without cellphones. And there were always phone booths in the streets, though the other person had to be at home for that to be of any use."

"This is really interesting," I said. "What else was different back then?"

"Well, we didn't have these electric kettles that

shut off by themselves when the water boils. We had a teakettle that we heated on the stove, with a whistle in the spout. When the water boiled, the kettle began to whistle loudly, and we knew to come shut off the fire."

"Oh," I said, "so that's what 'whistling like a teakettle' means! I saw that in books and never understood it till now."

"And we didn't have disposable plastic tablecloths," Bubby went on reminiscing. "If we wanted to cover the pretty Shabbos tablecloth so it wouldn't get dirty, we used thick heavy plastic that we had to wash after Shabbos."

"I guess things are much easier nowadays," I said.

"They sure are!" Bubby agreed. "What's that? Is someone knocking?"

She went to open the door, and I heard Chemda's voice. It sounded low and hesitant, not bright

and cheerful like yesterday. "Hello. How is Batya feeling?"

"Okay, Boruch Hashem," Bubby answered. "She's lying down and resting, like the doctor said."

"Can I come in and visit?"

"Wait a moment. I'll see if now is a good time."

Bubby came back into my room and said quietly, "It's Chemda. Should I invite her in?"

"No, tell her now is not a good time," I whispered back. "I'd rather go on talking with you, Bubby. It's so interesting."

And you know something? It wasn't just to get out of Chemda's visit. It was the truth! It really was interesting talking to Bubby about all kinds of things. We had a good time together until everyone came home for lunch.

"After lunch we'll stay here and play with you," Bentzi promised.

"But what will we play?" asked Tova. She had a point; we had forgotten to bring any games along with us.

Someone knocked on the door. Nadav and Chemda! I was afraid Chemda would ask again if she could come in, but instead they asked Bentzi and Tova to come outside with them. Chemda must have realized I didn't want her visiting me.

Bentzi and Tova were outside with them quite a while. When they came back in, they stole sideways glances in my direction, and I knew at once what they had been talking about.

"Go with them, it's okay," I said. "I'll be all right."

"Nadav wants to go hunting for the treasure again," said Bentzi, "but I—"

"I'll play with her," said Zaidy. "I can play a game as well as anyone!"

"But Zaidy, we didn't bring along any games,"

I said.

"Do we have paper? Pencils? Brains?" asked Zaidy. "Then we're all set!"

Bentzi and Tova went treasure-seeking. Bubby went for a walk with Amalya, and Zaidy and I played all kinds of games that he showed me, games that you need only paper and pencils and brains to play.

The time passed by swiftly, and suddenly the door flew open. Bentzi and Tova burst inside, crying excitedly, "Batya! You'll never believe what we found!"

I stared at them, dumbfounded. No, it couldn't be. This treasure — outside of Bentzi's imagination it was just a made-up story, wasn't it? So what were they saying? Why were they so excited?

"What? You... you really found... the treasure?"

10. What Nadav Found

You probably think I was overjoyed to hear the good news.

The fact is, it's hard to say exactly what I felt. I was glad, of course. I thought about our charity fund, and the dishwasher and camera and swimming lessons and rocking horse, and felt almost dizzy. But somehow I also felt disappointed and annoyed.

At long last there was an interesting adventure,

and what had seemed like a figment of Bentzi's overactive imagination turned out to be incredibly real — so why did I have to be left out? I wasn't there for the finding of the treasure, which must have been so exciting! I would have loved to be part of it. I pictured them searching among the bushes and suddenly finding a mysterious sack, or perhaps digging in the ground and suddenly hearing a hollow thud and discovering an ancient chest full of — of what?

Curiousity won out over all other feelings, and I asked eagerly, "What did you find? What is the treasure? Gold nuggets?Precious stones?Jewels?"

"No, you don't understand," said Tova. "We didn't find the treasure."

"You didn't?" I let out my breath and burst out laughing. All that excitement and happiness and disappointment and curiosity, all for nothing... "What **did** you find?" I asked. "Something interesting, at least? You look excited. Did you find an old well? A tall tower?An ostrich?"

"We didn't find the treasure," said Bentzi, "but we found something to do with it. Something that might lead us to the treasure!"

"I don't understand. Explain it clearly."

"I'm trying, but I don't know where to begin."

"Begin at the beginning and go on till you come to the end; then stop," said Zaidy cheerfully. "That's the advice of a great author."

"Some great author," Bentzi grumbled. "Real smart — begin at the beginning! The question is: What is the beginning?"

"The beginning is when you went out after lunch to seek the treasure," I said.

"Okay. So, it's like this: We went to the abandoned house and began searching the yard again, and suddenly Nadav thought of looking in the mailbox. There's an old-fashioned mailbox there, on a pole, and it wasn't locked."

"And he found an old envelope!" Tova burst out, jumping up and down with excitement. "You won't believe what was inside it!"

"You opened an envelope addressed to someone else?" I asked in disbelief. "Even if Alexander Stone died years ago, I don't think you should read his letters."

"Of course not, big sister dear. But this envelope wasn't addressed to him — it was addressed to us!" With a flourish, Bentzi pulled a yellowing envelope from his pocket. "Here, look what it says."

In faded letters, that had probably once been black but were now brownish, four words were written on the envelope: **To the Treasure-Seekers**.

"See?" Bentzi beamed. "The treasure-seekers — that's us!"

"I guess so," I had to admit. "And what's

inside?"

"A riddle. The answer to the riddle will lead us to the treasure!"

"Did you manage to solve it?"

"We didn't even try," said Tova.

"Why not?"

"We waited to show you, Batya, so you could try to solve it together with us!" Tova declared, and Bentzi handed me the envelope and said, "Bad enough you couldn't come treasure-seeking. At least you can do this together with us."

Now I knew exactly what I felt: happiness at having such a brother and sister. "Thanks," I said quietly. "That was very nice of you."

"We hadn't the heart to amuse ourselves with riddles," Bentzi said in a solemn voice, "while our beloved sister lay alone and suffering in a darkened chamber."

Actually, I had been with Zaidy in a brightly

sunlit room, and my foot hardly hurt at all when I didn't try to stand up. But I understood exactly what Bentzi meant, and I smiled gratefully at him.

"Besides, you're better than us at solving riddles," added Bentzi in his ordinary voice.

"Open it now!" Tova urged.

But I wanted to get things clear first. "Who put this in the mailbox?" I asked. "Alexander Stone, years ago? How could he know we'd look there?"

"He didn't know exactly who'd look, of course," said Bentzi, "but he left a letter so that if anyone came someday to seek the treasure, they'd have a starting point."

"It's because he was a spy. That's what Nadav said," added Tova.

"What's that got to do with it?"

"Nadav said it was just like him to do such a thing," Bentzi explained, "because he was such a cunning spy, always putting on an act and fooling people, never being open and straightforward. So he hid his treasure in such a roundabout way, with riddles you have to solve to get to it. And he put the letter in the natural place to put letters — in the mailbox."

"Come on, let's solve the riddle!" Tova cried impatiently.

11. A Riddle

"Okay, okay," I told Tova, who was hovering around me impatiently. "I'll read the riddle right away."

By now, I too was really curious. I took out the paper that was in the envelope and unfolded it carefully on the table. It looked like a page torn out of an old notebook, lined in pale blue. Here is what it said:

A Riddle

The treasure isn't just lying around —
Search for it where Yosef found.

"Hmmm… where Yosef found," I said slowly, trying to think. "Where Yosef found **what?** I guess he wasn't very good at rhyming, this Alexander Stone— that must be why he wrote such a funny sentence. Does it mean Yosef the son of Yaakov Avinu?"

"I guess so," said Bentzi. "Do you remember anything about Yosef finding something?"

"Yes, wait a minute, I'm trying to remember… His goblet! He sent servants to look for his goblet, right? And they found it in Binyomin's sack."

"Good for you, Batya!" Bentzi beamed. "You really listen in class. But what does it mean? Where does this clue tell us to look for the treasure?"

"Maybe it means we should look in a sack. Are

there sacks in the yard of the abandoned house?"

Bentzi and Tova tried to remember. "There are bushes, and old cardboard boxes, but I don't think there are any sacks," said Tova.

"Well, who said we have to look only near the abandoned house?" I asked. "The treasure could be anywhere in the village, couldn't it?"

"It could," agreed Bentzi, "but I don't think so. The spy wanted the treasure-seekers to find it in the end, right? The way should be clever and roundabout, true, but not impossible! So it makes sense that the treasure is hidden nearby."

"So if there aren't any sacks nearby, maybe it's something else to do with Yosef? What else did he look for?"

"His brothers!" cried Tova triumphantly.

"Wow!" Bentzi smiled at her. "I see you listen in class too. I'm really proud of both my sisters. Where did Yosef find his brothers? Do you remember that as well?"

"In a field?" Tova ventured uncertainly.

"There are plenty of fields around here, but how can we search in such a huge area?" I asked. "There must be a more practical solution to this riddle."

"My dear young scholars," Zaidy put in, "Yosef searched for his brothers in the fields, but finally found them in Dothan."

"Where's that?" asked Tova, but no one knew the answer.

"I don't think Dothan is the solution," I said, carefully refolding the paper and putting it back into the envelope. "I think you should go back to the abandoned house and look for sacks, or anything else to do with Yosef or Binyomin, and then—"

I broke off at the sound of knocking. Oh, no, could it be Chemda?

"If it's Chemda, tell her I need to rest," I

whispered to Bentzi and Tova.

But it was just Nadav by himself this time. Chemda must have given up on trying to see me.

"We're going to the abandoned house again," Bentzi told Nadav. "We thought we'd look for things that have to do with Yosef, the son of Yaakov Avinu. I'll explain on the way. Can you come along now?"

"Ummm... yes," said Nadav. He hesitated, then said, "So you solved the riddle? That's great! Good for you! Do you think we'll really find the treasure? Do you think Alexander Stone really used **all his money** to buy **diamonds**, and hid them away?"

His words rang a bell. All his money... buy diamonds... it conjured up a memory of sweet-smelling grass, soft breezes, Nadav telling us about a spy who bought diamonds with all his money, and Tova saying... What was Tova saying?

"Like the mean neighbor in *Yosef Mokir*

Shabbos," Tova said once again, just as she had said when she first heard Stone's story.

"That's it!" I cried. "It's Yosef Mokir Shabbos!"

"What?" Bentzi and Tova stared at me, confused.

I took the note out of the envelope and waved it eagerly at them. "Here, see? It says: 'Search for it where Yosef found.' It means Yosef from the story of Yosef Mokir Shabbos! Well, where did he find the diamond?"

"Inside a fish," Bentzi and Tova answered in chorus, and Tova asked, "Are there fish in the abandoned house?"

"There was something in the shape of a fish, I think," I said. "Or a picture of a fish... I can't remember exactly."

"We'll go look, and if we find the treasure we won't open it without you," Bentzi promised. "We'll bring it back and open it together."

12. Fishing

Bentzi and Tova went out to seek the treasure together with the twins. I stayed home, of course, with my tiresome sprained ankle. But they told me all about it afterwards, and I'll tell you everything as if I had been with them, okay? Because that way it'll be more interesting than just to report what they told me afterwards.

The abandoned house didn't look as scary as it had the first time. But it still looked mysterious, maybe even more than it had the first time. Now it looked like a house that concealed a treasure with puzzling clues leading to it.

"Batya said she remembers something in the shape of a fish, or a picture of a fish," said Tova, and everyone began roaming about the yard, looking carefully at the outer walls of the house, the front door, the windows, the fence, searching all over for anything fish-like.

"Here!" Tova called out suddenly, drawing out a colorful flyer from among the old cardboard boxes. "Look! A picture of a fish!"

Everyone gathered around her and looked. Indeed, between a picture of a bottle of wine and a picture of a package of salami, there appeared a picture of glassy-eyed carp, "at a special discount price."

"But this is just a thin piece of paper, not something you could hide a treasure in," said

Chemda.

"Yes, but maybe there's a clue here showing us where to look next," Tova suggested.

Bentzi took the flyer from her hand and examined it. "No, look, it says the date here, and it's just a few months back. Stone hid the treasure and the clues years ago!"

"The wind must have blown this into the yard," said Nadav. "Come, let's go on searching."

This time it was Bentzi who suddenly cried, "Here it is!"

Everyone hurried over. He was pointing at a large earthenware flowerpot that stood by the fence in the back yard. It had probably once been home to a blooming plant, but now contained nothing but dry earth. "It's shaped like a fish!" Bentzi explained, pointing out the pattern carved on the pot. "See, here's the head, and these are the scales."

"And here's the tail!" Tova joined in.

It really did look like a fish. Rather an odd fish, rounder than you'd expect, but definitely meant to be a fish.

"So let's look inside the flowerpot," said Nadav.

They began burrowing eagerly into the dry earth. Bentzi's heart beat quickly. Were there precious stones or rare jewels hidden in this common dirt?

"I found it!" Tova cried, holding up an envelope. Another ordinary envelope, just like the first one, except that this one was covered with dirt.

And now we're up to the part I was there for, instead of just hearing about.

"This is the treasure?" I said in disbelief, looking at the dirty envelope. I had imagined a heavy wooden chest full of shiny gold coins... What kind of treasure could be hidden in this plain old

envelope?

"Maybe there are diamonds inside," said Bentzi. "Even tiny diamonds are worth lots of money."

I felt the envelope. There seemed to be only a piece of paper inside — but could there be diamonds wrapped in it?

"We didn't open it, see?" said Tova. "We brought it back for you to open, because you couldn't be with us when we found it."

But what about Nadav and Chemda? I suddenly thought. Surely they would also love to be part of this exciting moment. It's because of me that they didn't come in with Bentzi and Tova, I know. Chemda knows I don't want to see her. But it's not fair that we should discover the treasure without them! If not for them we would never have even known the treasure existed!

So maybe we should call them in and open the envelope together?

It wasn't easy, not after what Chemda had done. After all, it was her fault I had missed all the excitement of finding the envelopes. But I knew it was the right thing to do. I swallowed my pride, which felt like a lump in my throat, and forced myself to say, "Why don't you go get Nadav and Chemda, and we'll all open this together?"

13. The Spreader of Light

"No," said Tova. "Chemda said they have to go now, and that we should open the envelope with you at home, they don't mind. Nu, Batya, just open it!"

Tova is just a little kid, after all, even though Bubby and Zaidy decided to count her as one of the big ones. She took Chemda's words at face value, not reading anything between the lines. But

I think Chemda's feelings are hurt, and that's why she's keeping her distance. What a pity. We could have had so much fun together during our stay, and afterwards maybe even been pen pals and kept in touch.

Maybe, just maybe, when I refused to see her, I had actually hoped she wouldn't give up so easily, but try again and again? Maybe I would have relented?

Oh, why waste time on such thoughts, when the treasure is right here in my hands? "Okay, I'm opening it," I said, and we all held our breath.

What was this? No diamonds, no precious stones. Just another page torn out of an old notebook, just like last time. We stared at it in disappointment for a moment, and then Bentzi said, "Of course! This isn't the treasure yet. Stone didn't want the hunt to be so easy. Each clue leads to yet another clue, until at the end we'll find the treasure itself."

I felt somewhat let down. I had been sure the treasure was already in our hands. But never mind. We wouldn't give up! We would go on, solving clue after clue, till we finally found the treasure. Maybe it was really better this way. Instead of just lying bored in bed, I had another riddle to figure out. It was a good way to pass the time.

"Well, let's get on with it," I said. "First of all we have to solve this riddle."

It was a short riddle, like last time. Just two lines:

The treasure is protected, by day and by night
Inside the dwelling of the spreader of light.

"What does it mean?" wondered Tova. "Dwelling means house, doesn't it? The abandoned house? But Nadav said it's dangerous to go inside, and anyway the door is locked."

"It's not the abandoned house," I said, "because that's not the dwelling of any spreader of light. It's a dark, empty house, and even when somebody did dwell there, it was just a spy who didn't do any light-spreading."

"How can you be so sure?" argued Bentzi. "Maybe he meant he spread light through his missions for the sake of the nation's safety."

"That doesn't sound right," I said. "Nobody calls spying 'light-spreading.' I think we should look for another house in the village, the home of someone who visits the poor and sick and gives them money and warm food and cheery words. In books that's always called 'spreading sunshine and light.'"

"How will we know who does that?" asked Tova.

"We can ask Nadav and Chemda," said Bentzi. "They're sure to know. But how can Stone have

hidden his treasure in somebody else's house without their knowing it? And how will we get into that house to search? They'll laugh at us if we try to explain, they'll never believe us. I'm telling you, grownups never believe me when I say things that sound like an adventure out of a book."

"Maybe a person like that, who's always spreading sunshine and light, will believe children who are telling the truth?" Tova suggested hopefully. "Even if it does sound like an adventure from a book?"

"That has nothing to do with it," I said. "Helping the poor is one thing, and believing what sounds like made-up stories is another thing entirely."

"In short," Bentzi summed up, "the treasure, or another clue leading to it, can't be in anyone's house."

"So why does it say 'inside the dwelling of the spreader of light'?"asked Tova.

Before we could come up with another solution, Zaidy called Bentzi to come along to shul with him, to daven Mincha and then learn together.

After Bentzi left, I tried to solve the riddle, but got nowhere.

And suddenly, while thinking about the riddle and the treasure, and about how Bentzi had said grownups never believed him when he said things that sounded like adventures out of books — a startling idea occurred to me. Not an answer to the riddle — something else entirely. A strange idea.

14. A Strange Idea

Could it really be possible? Hard to believe. But it could explain a lot... I didn't know what to think.

Grownups didn't believe his tales. So Bentzi had said. But I — I wasn't a grownup yet. I was just a child, even though I felt so much older than Tova. Could I have been led into believing something Bentzi had made up out of his imagination?

Yes. I couldn't deny it — there was something

odd about this whole treasure hunt thing. For years and years nobody had found the teasure, and here we had only to arrive in the village and clues started turning up. Had no one looked in the mailbox during all those years? And those riddles… They sounded so childish… Could a spy really have written them to lead people he didn't even know to a fortune?

Could Bentzi have thought it all up, written and hidden the riddles himself? It made me feel silly to think I had believed it was real. But maybe he had felt sorry for me because I couldn't go out, and that's why he decided to organize something exciting, to brighten up my dreary, empty hours.

The more I thought about it, the more it made sense. I thought of the time Bentzi had planned a surprise party for Tova. Remember? I told you all about it in The Amazing Adventures of Bentzi. To make Tova happy, Bentzi thought up something that disappointed her at first, before she knew what it was all about. Here it was the other way around, but the principle was the same. He wanted to cheer me up in my time of trouble, even if afterwards, when I knew what it was all about, I would be a little disappointed.

Bentzi, my wonderful brother! I felt a burst of fondness for him. What a heart of gold, always thinking of others! I resolved not to tell him I knew his secret. I would play along with him, try to solve the riddles and find the treasure. What kind of treasure could he be planning to hide at the end? Anyway, the first thing was to solve this riddle.

The treasure is protected, by day and by night
Inside the dwelling of the spreader of light.

What could it be? Tova and I tried again, but

we couldn't figure it out. "Never mind," I told her, thinking, Bentzi knows the answer anyway... He can always give us a hint.

Next morning Bubby and I went back to the clinic to have my ankle checked. Chemda's father volunteered to take us in his car again. "I asked Chemda to come along," he told us, "but she said she didn't feel like getting up early during vacation."

Oh! I felt myself blushing. What a shame. If I had been nicer to Chemda, maybe she would have felt like getting up early to come to the clinic with me. It's true that because of her I fell into the brook and sprained my ankle and missed out on so much. It was terribly annoying, but the more I thought about it, the more I felt I shouldn't be so mad at her. She had meant well, that was for sure. She thought I'd cross the brook easily, like she and Tova had, and have fun with them on the other side. It was a mistake to pester me about it and ignore my protests, but we all make mistakes sometimes, don't we? It's not as if she meant for me to get hurt.

The doctor was pleased with my progress. "Good, good," she said. "You don't need the bandage anymore. You can start walking again, but take it easy at first. Don't walk too far, and if you feel pain, stop and rest."

"Okay," I promised, overjoyed that I wouldn't have to stay home in bed anymore. I could make the most of the rest of our stay.

Bentzi and Tova were delighted when they heard the good news. "Now you can come with us to the abandoned house to seek the treasure!" Tova said.

"That's pretty far. The doctor said to take it easy at first."

"Anyway, we don't know if we should seek the treasure there or someplace else," said Bentzi. "Remember? We didn't figure out who the 'spreader of light' is. Maybe I'll go ask Nadav if he can think of anything."

Bentzi is a really good actor. To hear him talk, you'd never guess he made up that riddle himself, and knows the answer perfectly well.

15. To the Abandoned House

Bentzi went off to "ask Nadav," and I read the riddle again, racking my brains. Wouldn't it be great if I could surprise Bentzi and reach the solution myself, without the hints he'd pretend were Nadav's ideas?

But I couldn't do it. "Bubby, Zaidy, can you solve this riddle?" I asked. Bubby looked at it, wrinkling her forehead in concentration, and Zaidy asked,

"What is it exactly, something to do with that riddle about Yosef? Didn't Bentzi say something about a spy?"

"Yes, there's an abandoned house here," Tova began the tale. "Nobody lives there, but once upon a time a spy used to." She got all excited as she told of finding the first clue in the mailbox. I guess she's not in on Bentzi's secret. She obviously really believed what she was saying.

"Very interesting," said Zaidy. "Know what, maybe I'll ask Chananya what he can tell me about this abandoned house."

"Who's Chananya?" I asked.

"One of the oldest residents of Silver Brook. I met him in shul and we learned together. He's lived here all his life, he must know all about this abandoned house and your Mr. Stone."

"Yes, Zaidy, ask him!" I said. "I want to know if this whole treasure story is really true."

Tova looked at me wonderingly. "Batya, you know it's true! Here's Bubby right here looking at the riddle we found."

"Yes, but I can't figure it out," said Bubby.

Nobody could. I asked Mommy over the phone, when I called to tell her what the doctor had said, and she didn't know the answer either.

Then I decided to call Esti. I had told her when I sprained my ankle, so it was only right to let her know it was better now. I tried to read her the riddle, but she just said, "You know I'm no good at that kind of thing. So, are you having fun with that Chasida you told me about — the girl who lives in the village?"

"Not Chasida. Chemda."

"Oh, right. Chemda. I bet she came over all the time while you had to stay in bed. Just don't have such a good time with her that you forget me!" Esti laughed, and I tried to laugh along with her, but it

sounded so fake, I stopped right away.

"Don't worry," I told her, adding silently: If you only knew... You have nothing to worry about, because I have nothing to do with Chemda. We hardly got to know each other before we quarreled.

"Here's Bentzi coming back now!" Tova announced from her lookout at the window, and I told Esti goodbye and hung up.

"Nadav says we should look around the abandoned house again," said Bentzi. "See if we find anything that looks like the answer to the riddle, like we did last time with the fish."

Aha, I thought, and there you'll find a way to direct our attention to the place you hid the treasure, or the next clue...

"This time you can come too, Batya!" Tova said, beaming.

"I'm not sure Batya should walk so far today,"

said Bubby doubtfully. "The doctor said to take it easy at first."

"Please, Bubby!" I begged. "I'm dying to go out and be part of all the fun."

"Okay," Bubby relented, "but walk slowly, and if you feel it's a strain, stop and rest."

"I'll see to that," promised Bentzi. "Come on, let's find the dwelling of the spreader of light!"

We set out, with me walking slowly and carefully. What joy to use both feet again! I whispered thank you to Hashem for this wonderful gift.

"Where are Nadav and Chemda?" asked Tova.

"They said not to wait for them, they'll join us soon," said Bentzi. "It's better this way, because it'll take us a while to get there walking slowly like Bubby said."

So Chemda is still avoiding me. Still upset because I avoided her, I guess. I tried not to think about it, to just enjoy walking along the lovely paths of Silver Brook Village, smelling the flowers and bushes, hearing the birds chirping all around and the cows mooing in the distance.

"How's your foot, Batya?" Tova asked anxiously. "We're almost there. I can see the house already."

As we approached the neglected, overgrown yard, I suddenly knew the answer to the riddle. "Here!" I cried, pointing excitedly. "Here's the dwelling of the spreader of light!"

16. The Treasure

My foot was beginning to ache, even though we had walked really slowly, but I forgot the pain in the excitement of solving the riddle. "Look!" I said, pointing at a small lamppost that stood by the front door of the abandoned house. It was topped by a large plastic globe that was useful as well as decorative, protecting the light bulb inside from the weather. "The bulb is 'the spreader of light' and its 'dwelling' is this globe, that protects it by day and by night from rain and sun and whatever."

Bentzi beamed. "Batya, you're a genius!"

I almost retorted, "You made up this riddle yourself, so what's the big deal if I managed to solve it?" But then I thought: What difference does it make who thought up the riddle, Alexander Stone or my brother Bentzi? If I solved it, I solved it!

I smiled at Bentzi, and we all went over to the lamppost. Bentzi grasped the globe in both hands and began unscrewing it. Tova and I watched intently, holding our breath. What would we find inside? A treasure? Maybe the story of the treasure was true after all. Or would we just find another clue that Bentzi had hidden? It was so exciting to actually be there for the hunt, instead of just helping solve the riddles at home. I wouldn't have missed this for anything!

And why should Chemda miss it?

"Just a second, Bentzi," I said. "Shouldn't we wait for Nadav and Chemda and open this together?"

"Yes, but why aren't they here yet?" said Tova, looking back at the path we had arrived by. "We walked so slowly, I was sure they'd catch up with us."

"They said not to wait," said Bentzi, lifting off the globe. On the metal base where the light bulb should have been lay a small package, wrapped in shiny giftwrap.

"The treasure!" cried Tova, jumping up and down. "We found it at last! The clues were in plain old envelopes. Such a fancy package must be the treasure itself. Let's open it right now!"

But Bentzi said, "Wait. Do you hear what I hear?"

I listened carefully and heard steps approaching. Turning, I saw two figures coming nearer — Nadav and Chemda.

"Let's wait for them," I said, though I felt I couldn't bear to wait another second. Why does waiting always get harder near the end? Like when my aunt got married. I waited for the wedding for months, and enjoyed having something to look forward to. But on the wedding day, when we were waiting for it to be time to leave for the hall, every minute felt like forever.

Now I felt the same way. Just a few minutes ago I hadn't felt any special need to find the treasure immediately, but now that the package was right in front of us I could hardly wait a moment for Nadav and Chemda to arrive. But I had kept away from Chemda enough till now. Now I knew I must wait for her, and share the finding of the treasure with her.

In the meantime I looked around. Here was the mailbox, there the fish-shaped flowerpot. I tried to imagine what it was like discovering the envelopes in them, but my thoughts kept turning to Chemda. She would be here any second. What should I do? Act normal, as though nothing had happened? Apologize? Wait for her to apologize?

"We found it!" Bentzi called out to Nadav. Maybe everybody would start talking about the solution to the riddle and the package we had found even before they got into the yard, and I wouldn't have to actually say anything to Chemda.

But Chemda came straight over to me with her quick springing steps, her bright braids swinging behind her. "Why are you standing, Batya?" she asked, just as if nothing had happened between us. "Doesn't it hurt your foot?"

"Yes, it does hurt a little," I admitted, sitting down on the steps leading to the front door. I felt better right away. "Come, Chemda, sit here too," I said almost without thinking, moving aside to make room for her. Chemda hesitated for a moment, then sat down beside me.

"The moment has arrived!" Bentzi announced solemnly. "We are about to discover the long-lost treasure of the abandoned house."

With a flourish he lifted the package out of "the dwelling of the spreader of light" and waved it about in front of us. We all held our breath. The only sound heard in the expectant silence was the tearing of the giftwrap.

17. The Mystery Solved

"Why, it's a siddur," said Bentzi in a wondering tone.

"A siddur?" Tova echoed, amazed. "But where's the treasure?"

"And look what it says here!" Bentzi went on, handing me a beautiful sky-blue siddur, decorated with sparkling colored stones. On the cover, in gilt letters, was my name: Batya.

"How can it be?" Tova sounded surprised and confused. But I understood exactly what was going on, of course. Bentzi, who had thought up this whole treasure hunt to amuse me while I couldn't walk, had hidden a present for me at the end. How nice of him!

But Bentzi looked just as confused as Tova. "I don't understand," he muttered, staring wide-eyed at the siddur. "Is this the treasure?"

Why go on pretending? Did he really imagine that I'd go on believing the story of the spy? That I'd believe Stone had prepared a present years ago for a girl named Batya who would find the clues he had hidden?

"Bentzi," I said. "You can stop acting now. I understand everything. At first I really believed it was a real treasure the spy hid, but in the end I realized what was going on, and I was so glad—"

My words were suddenly cut off. Chemda, who

was sitting beside me on the front step, jumped up and hugged me. "Really, Batya?" she cried. "Were you really glad when you realized it? That's great! I wanted so much to make you happy!"

What? Suddenly I was as confused as Tova. What was Chemda saying? Wasn't it Bentzi behind the treasure hunt after all? Was it Chemda???

"I was so sorry you sprained your ankle because of me," said Chemda. "I planned to come over a lot and help you pass the time, but you weren't interested."

Oh! I felt myself blushing furiously, but Chemda went on as though she didn't notice, "So I tried to think of a different way to help you pass the time while you couldn't walk. I couldn't bear to think of you spending your precious vacation days lying bored in bed, and all because of me! And then I remembered this treasure story that you had taken such an interest in. I bought you this present,

סדור
בתיה
סדור
בתיה

and Nadav and I planned how we would hide envelopes with clues in the yard of the abandoned house and get you to look there, and in the end we would hide the present."

"And Bentzi?" I asked, still finding it difficult to get used to this new explanation. "Didn't Bentzi know anything?"

"No. Nadav decided not to tell him, so he wouldn't have to lie to you. We just wrote the riddles and hid the envelopes, without telling any lies. We never said it was the spy. Nadav only said it was **like** a cunning spy to think up such a plan."

"We found old, yellowing envelopes at home," Nadav said, "and we wrote on them with a marker that was partly dried up, so the letters would look faded."

"What? Chemda, was it you who organized this treasure hunt?" asked Tova in amazement. "It wasn't the spy? Is that why you always said to take the envelope home and let Batya open it?"

"Yes, of course, otherwise it would all have been for nothing. I did it all for Batya."

"You never said that was Chemda's idea!" I told Tova.

"Because she only said they had to go home now, and we could open it with you," Tova explained. "And Bentzi and I also thought you were missing out enough already, so we could at least let you open the envelopes."

"Nadav, it was you who suggested looking in the mailbox to start with, wasn't it?" Bentzi joined the conversation at last. "Now I'm beginning to understand... I'm flabbergasted."

"Yes, it just didn't occur to you to look there, so I had to bring it up myself," said Nadav. He laughed. "And afterwards, when you thought the riddle was about Yosef the son of Yaakov Avinu,

I had to think up some hints quick, to get you thinking about Yosef Mokir Shabbos, so you'd look for a fish." Suddenly he turned serious. "You aren't mad at us, are you, Bentzi?"

"Mad? Of course not! It was a terrific adventure, just the kind I like. Even a vacation in the country can be boring, if there's nothing special to do. Thanks to you we weren't bored for a moment!"

"I just wanted to cheer you up, Batya," said Chemda. "But then I began worrying that maybe you'd be disappointed in the end, when you saw it wasn't a real treasure."

"But it **is** a real treasure," I said. "And you, Chemda, are a real friend."

18. The Real Alexander Stone

"Thank you so much, Chemda!" I said. "And — I'm sorry. You organized all this for me, and I was just mad at you for nothing. It wasn't really your fault that I fell in the brook. You meant well."

"It was partly my fault," said Chemda. "I should have left you alone when I saw you didn't want to cross over. So let's forgive each other and be friends again! We still have a few days to have fun here together."

"And we believed you..." Tova muttered. I knew just how she felt. I had felt the same way myself when I first suspected the treasure hunt wasn't real. No one likes to feel they've been fooled. But Chemda had worked so hard to cheer me up, and I was already sorry for getting mad at her the last time she did something out of good intentions. And the time I spent at home had really been much more fun thanks to this treasure hunt!

"But you enjoyed it, didn't you?" I asked.

"Sure!" said Bentzi. "It's a pity it's not real after all, but in the meantime we had a great time. It was thrilling! How did you think it all up?"

We walked home slowly because of my ankle, and on the way Nadav and Chemda talked about how they had thought of the hiding places and the clues leading to them.

At home Zaidy said, "I have news for you!

Chananya told me all about the abandoned house."

"So is it true, what Nadav told us?" Bentzi asked eagerly. "We didn't find the treasure, but maybe the story's true anyway."

"Well... it's partly true," said Zaidy. "A rather small part... Apparently there is no treasure, but there really was an Alexander Stone living there years ago, who worked for the CIA."

"So he **was** a spy!"

"No, he was just an office worker," said Zaidy. "The CIA has offices just like any other organization. And he wasn't killed on any dangerous mission. He died of a heart attack."

"Then why doesn't anyone live in the house?" asked Bentzi. "Why is it empty and deserted?"

"Because after he died, his two sons—"

"Sons? Didn't he live alone?"

"He lived alone for many years, after his sons

grew up and moved away. His wife died long before him."

"I see how the rumor started," I said. "People got used to seeing him on his own, and they knew he worked in the CIA. All you need is a little imagination to fill in the blanks… There must have been a kid around here with an active imagination like Bentzi's, who thought up the whole story about the treasure."

"But why didn't the sons sell the house or rent it out?" asked Bentzi.

"There's a legal battle between them over the house. It's been dragging on for years in the courts. Each one of them claims the property is his, and meanwhile neither of them can use it."

"Why don't they just sell it and divide the money?" asked Tova.

Zaidy shrugged. "Could be all kinds of reasons."

"Yes," said Bentzi, setting his imagination to work. "Maybe one of them claims his father left the property only to him, and the other one says just the first one forged the will, or maybe just the signature, or—"

"Whatever the reason," I said, "it's too bad they can't reach an agreement and make peace. Because of this fight a perfectly good house has been standing there empty for years, doing nobody any good. Isn't it a pity?"

On the remaining days we went for long walks in the village, sometimes with Bubby and Zaidy and sometimes with Nadav and Chemda. Chemda and I spent hours together on the garden swing, swinging and talking. I was so glad we were friends again!

On the last day we exchanged addresses and promised to write. Then I found myself once more

in a van full of luggage, this time traveling in the opposite direction — homewards! Back to Mommy and Daddy, Moishy and Shmuel!

"I'll have so much to tell the members of the secret club," said Bentzi. "They'll never believe what an exciting adventure we had! And to think I worried it would be too quiet around here..."

"Look, the abandoned house!" cried Tova. We pressed our faces to the window for a last glimpse of the house that had looked so mysterious at first. Now it was just an empty house that no one could live in, because of a fight. Friendship and peace are the best treasure of all, I thought, and leafed through my new siddur, looking for Tefillas HaDerech. Goodbye, Silver Brook Village! Who knows, maybe we'll come back to you someday and have another adventure.